Giant Pandas

By Lisa M. Herrington

Children's Press®

An Imprint of Scholastic Inc.

Content Consultant
Columbus Zoo and Aquarium

Library of Congress Cataloging-in-Publication Data
Names: Herrington, Lisa M., author.
Title: Giant pandas/by Lisa M. Herrington.
Description: New York, NY: Children's Press, an imprint of Scholastic Inc., [2019] | Series: Nature's children | Includes index.
Identifiers: LCCN 2018023394| ISBN 9780531127162 (library binding) | ISBN 9780531134283 (paperback)
Subjects: LCSH: Giant panda—Juvenile literature.
Classification: LCC QL737.C27 H49 2019 | DDC 599.789—dc23

Design by Anna Tunick Tabachnik

Creative Direction: Judith E. Christ for Scholastic Inc.

Produced by Spooky Cheetah Press

Printed in Heshan, China   62

SCHOLASTIC, CHILDREN'S PRESS, NATURE'S CHILDREN™, and associated logos
are trademarks and/or registered trademarks of Scholastic Inc.

1 2 3 4 5 6 7 8 9 10 R 28 27 26 25 24 23 22 21 20 19

Scholastic Inc., 557 Broadway, New York, NY 10012.

Photographs ©: cover: Sylvain Cordier/Biosphoto/Minden Pictures; 1: GlobalP/iStockphoto; 4 leaf silo and throughout: stockgraphicdesigns.com; 4 top: Jim McMahon/Mapman®; 5 child silo: All-Silhouettes.com; 5 bottom: Edwin Giesbers/Nature Picture Library; 5 panda silo: Denis Sarbashev/Shutterstock; 6 panda silo and throughout: Evgeny Turaev/Shutterstock; 7: Pete Oxford/age fotostock; 8: Steve Bloom/Barcroft Media/Getty Images; 11: Edwin Giesbers/NPL/Minden Pictures; 12: Roni Rekomaa/REX/Shutterstock; 15: Ingo Arndt/Minden Pictures; 16: Will Burrard Lucas/NPL/Minden Pictures; 19: mrbfaust/iStockphoto; 20 top left: Tim Fitzharris/Minden Pictures; 20 top right: Paul Sawer/FLPA/Minden Pictures; 20 bottom left: Nick Garbutt/Superstock, Inc.; 20 bottom right: D. u. M. Sheldon/age fotostock; 23: Katherine Feng/Minden Pictures; 24: Katherine Feng/Minden Pictures; 27: Cyril Ruoso/Nature Picture Library; 28: Ami Vitale/Getty Images; 31: Prehistoric Fauna/Roman Uchytel; 32: Claude Balcaen/Biosphoto; 35: JOHANNES EISELE/AFP/Getty Images; 36: Katherine Feng/Minden Pictures; 39: ALAIN JOCARD/AFP/Getty Images; 40: Steve Bloom/Barcroft Media/Getty Images; 42 bottom: GlobalP/iStockphoto; 42 center left: Musat/iStockphoto; 42 center right: wrangel/iStockphoto; 42 top: Martin Mecnarowski/Shutterstock; 43 top right: anankkml/iStockphoto; 43 bottom right: Natalia Volkova/Dreamstime; 43 bottom left: Alexchered/Dreamstime; 43 top left: Dave King/Getty Images.

◀ **Cover image shows a giant panda in a bamboo forest in China.**

Table of Contents

Fact File..4

CHAPTER 1   **Beloved Bears**................................6
Home on the Misty Mountains................9
Pandas Up Close................................10
Famous Fur................................13

CHAPTER 2   **A Panda's Life**................................14
Sounds and Scents................................17
Something to Chew On................18
Staying Safe................................21

CHAPTER 3   **A Baby Is Born**................................22
Caring for Cubs................................25
Growing Up Panda................................26
Venturing Off................................29

CHAPTER 4   **The Bear Family**................................30
Welcome to the Neighborhood................33

CHAPTER 5   **Protecting Pandas**................................34
Reserves to the Rescue................................37
Stars of the Zoo................................38
The Future of Pandas................................41

Giant Panda Family Tree................................42
Words to Know................................44
Find Out More................................46
Facts for Now................................46
Index................................47
About the Author................................48

Fact File: Giant Pandas

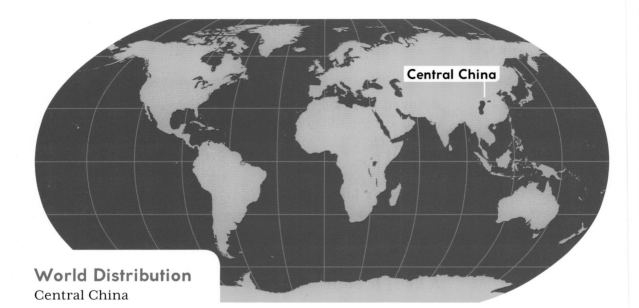

Central China

World Distribution
Central China

Habitat
Cool, rainy mountain forests where bamboo grows plentifully

Habits
Live mostly alone; spend their days eating bamboo and sleeping; skilled tree climbers; communicate through sound and scent

Diet
Mainly bamboo plants; occasionally grass, fruit, and small animals

Distinctive Features
Large, powerful bodies covered in thick black-and-white fur; strong jaws and teeth for chewing bamboo; front paws with an extra wrist bone for grasping bamboo

Fast Fact
Wild pandas sleep in hollow logs or tree stumps.

Average Size

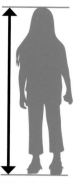

4 ft. 6 in.
(1.4 m)

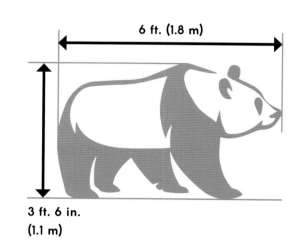

6 ft. (1.8 m)

3 ft. 6 in.
(1.1 m)

Human (age 10)

Panda (adult)

◀ In Chinese, pandas are called big bear cats. Their pupils are shaped like a cat's.

CHAPTER 1

Beloved Bears

A heavy mist hangs over the mountains. Perched high in a tree, a cute, pudgy-faced creature peers through the leaves and clambers down the branches. It lumbers past a rocky stream, stops for a sip of water, and settles into a thick patch of grass. The hungry animal grabs a handful of **bamboo** with its front paws and starts to eat. This tough, tasty plant is a panda's favorite food.

Giant pandas are unusual bears known for their remarkable black-and-white fur. In the wild, they live only in **remote** forests in central China where bamboo thrives.

People around the world adore pandas. They are considered national treasures in China. They attract large crowds at zoos. They have become symbols of peace, friendship, and wildlife **conservation**. Giant pandas were once on the edge of **extinction**, but people have been working to save these beloved bears.

▶ While eating, pandas often sit upright to free up their front paws so they can grab bamboo.

Home on the Misty Mountains

Long ago, giant pandas were widespread throughout eastern and southern China. But over time, their habitat shrank as people cut down trees for wood and farmland.

Today, giant pandas live in moist forests on six mountain ranges in central China. The weather there is cool, damp, and rainy. It is a humid place—each year, about 50 inches (127 centimeters) of rain and snow fall. Bamboo does well in these conditions, growing among the trees.

The cloud-covered mountains pandas inhabit rise between 5,000 and 10,000 feet (1,524 and 3,048 meters). In spring, pandas are surrounded by rhododendrons and other flowers that sprinkle the slopes. In summer, pandas live high in the mountains. But unlike other bears, pandas do not hibernate during the snowy winter. Bamboo isn't nutritious enough for them to store up body fat for a long winter's rest. Pandas need to continue to eat. In winter, they move down the slopes where it is warmer.

◀ A panda relies on its strong climbing ability to survive in its mountain home.

Pandas Up Close

Giant pandas have bulky, bearlike bodies with large heads, round ears, and short legs. They grow to about the size of an American black bear. Males weigh 220 to 300 pounds (99.8 to 136.1 kilograms), and are slightly bigger than females.

When it comes to bamboo, pandas can't get enough. This plant is so strong that it is hard to cut with an ax. But pandas have special adaptations that allow them to easily survive on it. Behind the pandas' chubby cheeks are powerful jaw muscles and 42 strong teeth. Pandas use their sharp front teeth to chew through bamboo's hard outer layers to get to the juicy insides. They use their flat back teeth to crush the woody stalks.

Pandas also have four paws, each with five sharp claws. An extra bone on their front paws functions like a thumb to grasp bamboo.

Fast Fact
Pandas walk pigeon-toed with their front paws turned inward.

Short, Thick Legs
let pandas travel close to the ground through dense forests.

Black Fur

is found on the shoulders, legs, ears. and around the eyes.

Cheek Muscles

enable the panda to chew through more than 600 bamboo stems a day.

Teeth and Jaws

are strong enough to chomp an aluminum dish into tiny pieces.

Sharp Claws

resemble fingers to help the panda grasp bamboo.

Famous Fur

With their black-and-white fur, giant pandas are one of the most recognizable animals on the planet. No one knows for sure why giant pandas have these unique markings. Some scientists think the colors act as camouflage. In the forest, pandas' markings make them difficult to spot among the sunlight and shadows. In winter, the pattern helps pandas blend into their snowy and rocky mountain habitat. Other scientists think pandas' colors may help them find each other to mate.

Although a panda's coat looks like it is soft and cuddly, it actually feels a lot like a sheep's wool. The panda's thick, oily fur is waterproof and keeps the bear warm in its cold, wet home. Water runs off the fur so the panda stays dry.

◀ Distinct black-and-white markings help pandas hide near snow and rocks.

A Panda's Life

Giant pandas mostly live alone except for when they are mating or when a female is raising her young. They spend their days **foraging**, eating, and sleeping.

Pandas tend to wander slowly because they have heavy bodies. But they can move at a fast trot. Despite their size, pandas are surprisingly flexible. They are expert tree climbers, good swimmers, and can even do somersaults.

The area where a giant panda lives is called its home range. The size of the range depends on how much food is available. It is typically about 2 square miles (5.2 square kilometers). A giant panda doesn't have a permanent home within its range. It may nap in caves or high in trees. Pandas also climb trees to escape danger.

▶ Giant pandas may look clumsy, but they have impressive acrobatic skills.

Fast Fact
Pandas talk to
each other with
11 different calls.

Sounds and Scents

Giant pandas communicate with one another through sounds and scents. They sound like sheep bleating when they make friendly greetings. In spring, they can be noisy when they are looking for a mate. Pandas' chirps and barks carry through the forest. They sometimes growl when they are angry. They also honk, chomp, and squeal.

These big bears have an excellent sense of smell, too. Their powerful noses can detect another panda's scent up to 18 mi. (29.1 km) away. Pandas leave their scent behind to mark their area or to attract a mate.

A giant panda's short tail protects its scent glands. A panda keeps its tail tucked close to its body. It uses its tail to rub the odor from its scent glands onto rocks, tree trunks, bamboo, and bushes. A male panda may even do a handstand to leave its scent higher on a tree.

◀ A male leaves his scent on a tree to communicate with other pandas.

17

Something to Chew On

Imagine eating the same food for breakfast, lunch, and dinner every day. That's exactly what giant pandas do! Their diet is 99 percent bamboo. They occasionally eat grass, fruits, and small animals, but they would starve without bamboo.

Bamboo is filled with fiber and is hard to digest. Most of the bamboo passes through a panda's body as waste. That's why these big bears spend half the day— about 12 hours—munching away on this tough plant. Pandas eat anywhere from 25 to 85 lb. (11.8 to 38.6 kg) of bamboo a day. That would be like you eating about 20 to 85 heads of lettuce!

There are different kinds of bamboo, but pandas eat just the few types that grow in their home range. The animals have special protective linings in their throats and stomachs so the splintery bamboo doesn't hurt them when they swallow it.

▶ Giant pandas use their powerful teeth and jaws to crush thick bamboo stalks.

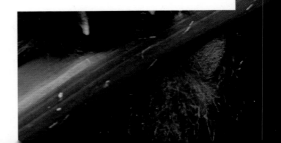

Tiger

▶ Tigers used to be a threat to cubs, but they no longer live in the same habitat.

Snow Leopard

▶ Snow leopards can catch large animals but are known to hunt panda cubs, too.

Dhole

Panda cubs are slow, which makes them a target for the fast dhole.

Yellow-Throated Marten

Martens generally eat fruits and small mammals, and occasionally, panda cubs.

Staying Safe

Because giant pandas are large, powerful bears, they have few natural **predators** in the wild. However, some animals like snow leopards, yellow-throated martens, and wild dogs will **prey** on panda babies. When a mother panda is off feasting on bamboo, her cub usually hides in a tree away from danger. But hiding places are not always safe . . . This is when predators attack baby pandas.

Predators don't want to mess with panda moms, though. Mother pandas are very protective of their cubs. Although pandas are generally peaceful creatures, they can make themselves look fierce and will defend themselves against attackers.

Just like other bears, pandas have sharp claws and powerful bites. When threatened, they may stare down their opponent and growl. Some scientists think the tear-shaped black fur around a panda's eyes may help scare off enemies.

◀ Some animals may try to make a meal out of young pandas.

CHAPTER 3

A Baby Is Born

Pandas' mating season takes place in spring. Female pandas give birth every two years. To attract a mate, a female makes calls and marks trees with special scents. This lets male pandas know she is ready to mate. Sometimes, males fight over a female. After mating, the male panda goes off on his own.

The female panda is pregnant for three to five months. In August or September, she finds a warm, safe **den** in the base of a hollow tree or a cave to give birth. She normally gives birth to one baby. If she does have twins, only one will survive.

Newborn pandas, called cubs, are tiny. They're only about the size of a stick of butter. The newborns measure about 6 in. (15.2 cm) long and weigh just 3 to 5 ounces (85 to 141.7 grams). A newborn panda is one of the smallest **mammals** relative to its mother's size. A mother panda is 900 times larger than her newborn. To compare, a human mom is only about 18 times larger than her baby.

▶ Newborn pandas are born pink, blind, and hairless.

Fast Fact
Newborn pandas spend their early days crying and squeaking.

Caring for Cubs

Newborn panda cubs are helpless. They depend on their mother entirely for survival. The female panda raises the baby alone. She may go days—or even weeks—without eating or drinking so she doesn't have to leave her cub.

A mother panda instantly forms a close **bond** with her cub. She tenderly cares for and **nurses** her baby. Like all mammals, baby pandas need their mother's milk for nourishment to grow. The mother snuggles and cradles her cub, usually in her giant paw close to her chest. She has to be careful not to accidentally crush her cub. She licks the baby clean. She keeps it warm and dry. When the mother moves around, she carries her baby in her mouth.

By the time the baby is two to three weeks old, it starts to grow black patches of fur. When the cub is about eight weeks old, it finally opens its eyes.

◀ A mother panda snuggles her cub to keep it warm.

Growing Up Panda

After two months, the cub begins to crawl. It is now the size of a human newborn. Soon, its teeth appear. When it is three months old, the cub takes its first wobbly steps, sometimes falling down. Just like children, panda cubs are curious and playful. They love to roll in the grass and climb on their mother.

By the time it is six months old, the cub is ready to explore the forest with its mother. The female panda stays close by the cub and teaches her baby everything it needs to know about surviving in the wild. The cub will learn how to bite bamboo and use its claws to climb trees to stay safe from danger.

The cub starts to **wean** from nursing at nine months old and starts eating bamboo. At about one year old, the tiny panda that was once the size of a pinecone will weigh almost as much as an eight-year-old human child.

▶ At six months old, this panda can climb trees using its claws and front legs.

Venturing Off

The young panda stays with its mother until it is two to three years old. By then, the panda is independent and can live by itself. When it heads off, it will find its own home range.

Now on its own, the young panda will be ready to mate when it is four to eight years old. The life cycle will begin anew.

The mother panda will soon mate again and have another baby. During her life, she will raise only five to eight cubs. These low birth rates make it harder for the panda **population** to increase when threatened.

In the wild, giant pandas live about 14 to 20 years. They may die from disease, old age, or lack of food because of habitat loss. Others may be hunted or killed by predators. Sometimes, they get caught in traps that are meant for musk deer and other animals. Pandas living under human care can live for 25 to 30 years.

◄ In their bamboo forests, pandas need streams nearby for drinking water.

CHAPTER 4

The Bear Family

For a long time, scientists debated whether giant pandas were related to bears or raccoons. Now we know: Giant pandas are one of eight kinds of bears that live around the world.

Scientists don't know for sure how giant pandas developed, but they think bears came from ancient plant- and meat-eating **ancestors** that lived about 23 million years ago. The ancestors of giant pandas may have split off into their own **species** about 12 to 18 million years ago. One of the giant panda's earliest relatives was a smaller bearlike creature called *Kretzoiarctos beatrix* or *K. beatrix*.

Giant pandas have roamed Earth for a long time— nearly 3 million years. During that time, Earth likely went through an Ice Age. The planet was much colder than today. Bamboo grew well in these temperatures. A smaller panda called *Ailuropoda microta* may have descended from those ancient relatives and developed into the pandas we know today.

▶ **This is an artist's rendering of the extinct *Ailuropoda microta*.**

Welcome to the Neighborhood

Giant pandas share their mountain habitat with many other fascinating creatures. Golden snub-nosed monkeys leap through the treetops. Mountain sheep climb the rugged hills. Golden eagles and colorful birds soar through the sky. And red pandas, which live in trees, sometimes wrap their bushy tails around themselves to stay warm.

Giant pandas and red pandas have a lot in common. They not only share an overlapping habitat and have a similar name, but they also have a preference for the same food— bamboo. Both animals also have an extra bone on their front paws that functions like a thumb for feeding on bamboo.

Despite all their similarities, giant pandas and red pandas are not relatives. After much research, scientists placed red pandas in their own family. They believe these reddish creatures are related to raccoons and skunks. The red panda certainly looks like it could be the cousin of a raccoon!

◀ A red panda is about the size of a house cat.

CHAPTER 5

Protecting Pandas

About 1.4 billion people live in China. As the human population grew, pandas were pushed from the lowlands into the mountains. Many of their forests were cut down to make room for homes, farms, and roads. These forests have been broken apart, making it difficult for pandas to mate and find food.

Bamboo is one of the world's fastest-growing plants. But about every 60 years, it goes through a die-off. As bamboo dies, it drops seeds that eventually grow into new plants. However, it takes a long time—10 to 15 years—for new bamboo to grow.

In the past, pandas would move to a new area to eat after a bamboo die-off. But today, with less forested lands, many pandas starve after die-offs. The Chinese government and conservation groups are working to solve the problem by connecting pockets of the pandas' broken forest habitat.

▶ As people chop down bamboo for roads, pandas lose their habitat.

Reserves to the Rescue

Today, giant pandas in China live mainly in safe areas called nature **reserves**. They are like national parks in the United States.

More than two-thirds of pandas in the wild live in China's 67 reserves, which are protected by law. The pandas there can't be harmed or hunted. Some people called **poachers** illegally hunt pandas for their fur, which can be sold for more than $40,000 a piece. The poachers can go to prison if they are caught.

Some reserves have research centers where scientists study panda behavior to learn more about them. **Breeding** programs at some centers help pandas have babies and boost their population. Many cubs have been born at China's Wolong (WOO-long) Panda Reserve.

As they observe and care for cubs, scientists may wear panda costumes and make themselves smell like the bears. They want the cubs to learn to be wild animals and not to get comfortable around humans. They hope to one day release more of these pandas back into the wild.

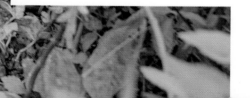

◄ Caretakers wear panda costumes while placing a collar on a panda.

Stars of the Zoo

About 300 pandas live under human care, mostly in breeding centers but also in zoos. The money from zoos supports pandas in the wild.

China loans pandas to zoos around the world. In 1972, giant pandas were brought to the United States from China to live at the National Zoo in Washington, D.C. It is one of four zoos in the United States that have pandas on loan from China.

Pandas sometimes give birth at zoos. The zoos have playgrounds for pandas to climb and play. Pandas not only eat bamboo at zoos, but they also feed on other foods like carrots, apple slices, yams, and even ice pops.

Zookeepers study pandas, take notes, and work closely with scientists in China. They learn as much as they can about these fascinating animals so they can help them survive in the wild.

▶ Pandas are one of the most popular attractions at zoos.

The Future of Pandas

Giant pandas are rare bears. These mysterious creatures are hard for scientists to find in the forest. Tracking them isn't easy. Scientists have a method that works, though: They study panda poop to help count how many live in a certain area. They also measure chewed-up bamboo sticks and follow pandas' footprints. Researchers also use **satellite** technology to help track and monitor pandas.

A lot of people have worked to save pandas. And it's paying off. Although there are only an estimated 1,864 pandas in the wild, their numbers are on the rise.

As giant pandas slowly make a comeback, scientists say there is still a lot of work to be done. Protecting the habitat of giant pandas also helps other animals that share the land. Many people—including kids who raise awareness—continue to do their part to ensure the survival of these beautiful bears.

◀ Pandas living under human care are more likely to have twins than those living in the wild.

Giant Panda Family Tree

Giant pandas belong to the bear family called *Ursidae*. All the members of this family share a common ancestor—*Ursavus* that lived 2.3 to 5.3 million years ago. This diagram shows how giant pandas are related to the other seven members of the bear family. The closer together two animals are on the tree, the more similar they are.

Sloth Bears
shaggy-coated bears that mainly eat termites and ants

Andean Bears
shaggy bears also called spectacled bears for the white rings of fur around their eyes, which can look like glasses

Sun Bears
small bears that get their name from the golden or white patch on their chests

Giant Pandas
black-and-white bears that live only in China and feed primarily on bamboo plants

Ancestor of all Bears

Note: Animal photos are not to scale.

**American
Black Bears**
medium-sized
bears that are
excellent tree
climbers

**Asiatic Black
Bears**
medium-sized
bears in Asia that
are known as moon
bears or white-
chested bears

Polar Bears
large bears with
thick, white fur
that live in the
icy-cold Arctic and
hunt seals

Brown Bears
huge bears that
are found in parts
of North America,
Europe, and Asia

43

Words to Know

A .... **adaptations** *(ad-ap-TAY-shuns)* changes a living thing goes through so it fits in better within its environment

ancestors *(ANN-ses-turs)* family members who lived long ago

B .... **bamboo** *(bam-BOO)* a tropical plant with a tall, woody stem

bond *(BAHND)* close connection with or strong feelings for someone

breeding *(BREED-ing)* to keep animals or plants under controlled conditions so they produce more and better quality offspring

C .... **camouflage** *(KAM-uh-flahzh)* a disguise or a natural coloring that allows animals, people, or objects to hide by making them look like their surroundings

conservation *(kahn-sur-VAY-shun)* protecting valuable things, especially forests, wildlife, or natural resources

D .... **den** *(DEN)* the home of a wild animal

E .... **extinction** *(ik-STINGKT-shun)* the act of killing off a species

F .... **foraging** *(FOR-ij-ing)* going in search of food

G .... **glands** *(GLANDZ)* organs in the body that produce or release natural chemicals

H .... **habitat** *(HAB-i-tat)* the place where an animal or plant is usually found

hibernate *(HYE-bur-nayt)* when animals hibernate, they sleep for the entire winter; this protects them and helps them survive when the temperatures are cold and food is hard to find

M......... **mammals** *(MAM-uhlz)* warm-blooded animals that have hair or fur and usually give birth to live babies; female mammals produce milk to feed their young

mate *(MATE)* to join together for breeding

N......... **nurses** *(NURS-ez)* drinks milk from a breast

P......... **poachers** *(POHCH-uhrz)* people who hunt or fish illegally on someone else's property

population *(pahp-yuh-LAY-shuhn)* all members of a species living in a certain place

predators *(PRED-uh-tuhrs)* animals that live by hunting other animals for food

prey *(PRAY)* when an animal hunts another animal for food

R......... **remote** *(ri-MOHT)* secluded or isolated

reserves *(ri-ZURVZ)* protected places where hunting is not allowed and where animals can live and breed safely

S......... **satellite** *(SAT-uh-lite)* spacecraft that is sent into orbit around the earth, the moon, or another heavenly body

species *(SPEE-sheez)* one of the groups into which animals and plants are divided; members of the same species can mate and have offspring

W......... **wean** *(WEEN)* stop drinking mother's milk to eat other foods instead

Find Out More

BOOKS

- Furstinger, Nancy. *Giant Pandas*. Mankato, MN: The Child's World, 2016.
- Jazynka, Kitson and Raven-Ellison, Daniel. *Mission: Panda Rescue*. Washington, D.C.: National Geographic Society, 2016.
- Murray, Julie. *Giant Pandas*. Minneapolis, MN: ABDO Publishing Company, 2013.

WEB PAGES

- www.worldwildlife.org/species/giant-panda

  The World Wildlife Foundation's comprehensive site has valuable information about giant pandas including the threats they face and ongoing conservation efforts.
- http://kids.sandiegozoo.org/animals/giant-panda

  The San Diego Zoo offers fun, detailed facts about giant pandas, information about its pandas, live videos from its panda cams, and ways kids can make a difference.
- https://nationalzoo.si.edu/animals/giant-panda

  The National Zoo's site is packed with awesome panda info and has links to frequently asked questions and amazing live footage from its panda cams.

Facts for Now

Visit this Scholastic Web site for more information on giant pandas: **www.factsfornow.scholastic.com** Enter the keywords Giant Pandas

Index

A

acrobatic skills 14, *15*

adaptations................................10

Ailuropoda microta 30, *31*

ancestors 30, *31*, 42

appearance 10, *11*, *12*, 13

B

bamboo 4, 6, *7*, 9, 10, 11, 17, 18, *19*, 21, 26, 28, 29, 30, 33, 34, *35*, 38, 41

birth rate 29

birthing.........................22, *23*, 38

bonding.............................. 25

breeding programs 37

C

camouflage *12*, 13

Chinese name 5

claws 10, *11*, 21, 26, *27*

climbing ability.................*8*, 9, 14, *15*, 26, *27*, 38

communication *16*, 17

conservation efforts.............6, 34, 41

cubs.................. 21, 22, *23*, 24, 25, 26, *27*, 28, 29, 37, *40*

D

dens 22

diet...........................4, 18, 25, 29, 38

distribution 4, 9

E

extinction 6

F

foraging.......................................14

fur.....................4, 6, *11*, 13, 21, 25, 37

future of pandas 41

H

habitat..................4, 6, *8*, 9, 13, 33, 34, *35*, *36*, 37, 41

hibernation 9

home range 14, 18, 29

human interactions 29, 34, *35*, *36*, 37, 38, *39*, 41

L

life expectancy............................ 29

M

mating.................... 13, 17, 22, 29, 34

milk.. 25

Index (continued)

N

nature reserves *36*, 37

nursing 25, 26

P

poachers 37

population 29, 41

predators *20*, 21, 29

R

red pandas *32*, 33

relatives 30, *32*, 33, *42*, *43*

S

satellite technology 41

scent glands *16*, 17

senses 17

size and weight 5, 10, 22

sleeping habits 4

T

threats *20*, 21, 29, 37

W

weaning 26

Wolong Panda Reserve 37

Z

zoos 38, *39*

About the Author

Lisa M. Herrington has written many books for kids. From ferocious wolves to adorable pandas, she loves learning about different animals. Lisa especially enjoyed getting to see giant pandas up-close at the San Diego Zoo. She lives in Trumbull, Connecticut—far from any wild pandas—with her husband, Ryan, and daughter, Caroline.